POETRY FOR THE PEOPLE

BY JEREMY PARKER

1.Broken promises!

Broken promises!

Broken lives!

Broken dreams!

Can't rely on others!

Or so it seems!

2.Drip of poison

Only takes one drip of poison

To feed an innocent mind

Bitter lies cant take away the memories

Of all our good times!

3. Darkness!

THERE IS NO LIGHT IN MY DAY

With every breath that I take

I have no escape

Some people have gone but the memories remain

Nether the less the pain stays the same

Until the sun shines agin again

And the darkness fades

The sun will rise when I see you again!

4.Abuse!

There are no words!

Only a mind full of silence

I will suffer know more

From a father's violence!

5.Absence!

 Absence makes the heart grow fonder

All that's left is to sit and wonder

All the time I lost watching you grow!

Losing you three a bitter pill to swallow!

6.FLAMES IN THE FIRE!

We were two flames in the fire

We burned together

The fire died out

After the day, your feelings were revoked

Maybe on your own smoke you choke!

7.LUCKY GUY.

If I was lucky enough to meet a girl

I hope we would walk together

If she would hold my hand

It would be just grand

As we walked on the beach

We would draw our names in a heart the sand!

8.VALENTINES DAY!

On valentine's day!

I wish you were mine!

Shower you with affection

Feed you chocolate and wine

Show you plenty affection

Give you my time

You are my special lady

That is always on my mind

Your beautiful eyes

Your so kind so pure

The luckiest person alive that is for sure!

9.CARE

If you are feeling low

Just reach out

Someone will come

Because around the corner

There is someone who will truly understand

To give you the helping hand

There is always someone to care

You are not a burden

Troubles can be shared

Don't be alone

You have a friend

Your lifes worth living

It's not the end.

10.TOO MANY TEARS.

These last few years

I have cried too many tears

Time to live my life

A whole fresh start

A brand-new year

Time to be happy

No more sadness in my heart

11.THE LIES

Just one last lie

Was just enough

To say our goodbyes

12.FREEDOM.

Unshackled my chains

Broke free from the control

I can now smile again

That im free from their hold

13.MISTAKES

Past mistakes have gone

And torturing yourself no good for your health

The demons in your past trying to destroy your soul

Remember happyness not money is real true wealth

Give yourself a break

Ignore people that judge

And getting this far has took sheer stealth

14.BLESSING

Were you a blessing?

Were you a curse?

I dedicated my life

Putting you first

I was cast aside

Not what I deserved

Just thrown out like trash.

15.POPPY DAY.

They fought for our freedom

They laid down their lives

With courage and honour

A real sacrifice

So just spare a moment

To remember the fallen

On rememberance day

Lest we forget.

16.HURT

The way I am feeling

it is not a choice

Stirring up demons

Sometimes they are silent

Sometimes they have a voice

17.SAD FACE

Sick of my sad face

Cannot wait for this year to end

Minds so messed up

You cannot comprehend

So, get me on a plane

On my own or with a friend.

18.DRUNK

I drank myself to the bottom

Scraping myself off the floor

To forget my life

Nobody had my back

Didn't tke much to bring me down

I made myself look stupid

Got used by others

What a clown

I took control

Rose above it all

What a shit show

19.SOMETHING POSITIVE

Waiting for something positive

Just sat in the dark

Just comprehending

Waiting for negative thoughts to subside away

I keep telling myself

Maybe just one more day

Waiting for tomorrow is an energy drain

Waiting and waiting

For a day free of pain

20.ALL THE YEARS

Sat here writing down my fears

In an ocean full of tears

Cracking open a bottle

Looking back on the years

All the years of hurt

When I was down on my knees

There were no warning signs

The thoughts in my head

Were just tricks of my mind

If I say its all gone away you know its all just a lie

I threw the towel in the ring

I gave up on my life

Threw it all away on a wim

Because my heart was drowning in my tears

21.TEAR ME APART

Trying to tear me apart with hurtful words

You should not say

No sorrow or regret

You tossed me away

You don't do forgiveness

But what can I say

It never was your fault anyway

22.FALL FROM GRACE

Staring into space

Nobody there to stop my fall from grace

Trying to forget all my sadness and frustration

I don't belong in this place

23.weight of the world

When the weight of the world is on your shoulder

And you are walking round dragging giant boulders

Staring into a blank space

No thoughts on your mind

Just that time and place

24.MEMORY OF YOU

My memory of you will never fade

A special place in my heart

Each day

As time passes by

You I will never forget

I know you are not here anymore

But the time we had together will never be forgot

Things put into perspective

What is important and what is not

I will miss you for the rest of my life

Each day

Wishing you was alive

But I will know you are looking down saying chin up son

Have a smile not a frown

25.LIFE FOR GRANTED

Everyone can take life for granted

If you ever feel nobody cares

Stop and stare take a good look around you on the street

All the homeless people

With nothing to eat

Starving in the cold

With no coat on their back

No shoes on their feet

Just remember your going to home that's full of heat

Think for a minute

At exactly what you have got

When you turn off the light at night

And get into your warm bed at night

Think about the people in the freezing cold

That everyones forgot

26.ADDICTIVE LADY

Good looking lady

Infectious kind of smile

She drives me crazy

She makes me feel alive

Hoping one day I can make her mine

27.HATE

I have only hate for myself

I have no hatred for nobody else

Hate of the way I am

Hate of feeling alone

Hate at the way im treat

Hate for the life I have

Hate myself for being me

But guess that's what is meant to be

Hating myself guess its my fate

Nothing gets better

Not in my head I know its too late

28.DROWNING

Drowning in my fears

Bloodstained tears

An emotional mess

My physical state

Energy drained

Battling my own demons

For my own mental cause

Just an emotional whore

Rotten to the core

Too many times I broke my own laws

A rebel for my cause

A cruel life has led me to this fate

It tore my heart apart

Something I could not contemplate

It is hard to breathe when your heads full of hate.

29. THE FUTURE

Don't look at the nightmares in your past

Try to live your life and have a blast

Don't look at your days wondering why

Look to the future and wear a smile

Be proud of who you are and how far you have come

Look for the positives

No time to be glum

You will get there in the end

Either on your own

Or with the help of a friend

But remember you are human

And nobodys perfect

So, live your life as someone famous said

Your bloody worth it

30. BETTER DAY AHEAD

Don't you think life is like weather

Rain cant rain on you forever

After every storm

The sun comes out

And the dark clouds go

And on the horizon a brighter day ahead

31 TRYING TO PLEASE OTHERS

Trying too hard to please others

When you should be trying harder to please yourself

Only have one life to live

So much to offer

So much to give

But giving to the wrong person is not good for your health

Life has been a struggle

Time now to take care of yourself

To come back stronger

Full of stealth

32.SELF CONTROL

Mind is numb

No heart no soul

Nothing has any meaning not for me anymore

Lockdown for me

Closing the curtains locking the door

My troubles my struggles my thoughts in my head

Today there will be knocks

Leave me alone I am staying in bed

Please be kind leave a message instead.

33 WEMBLEY WAY.

July the 11th is the day

When England walk down Wembley way

Beating the Italians will be no easy feat

And Jordan pickford keeping that clean sheet

It has benn far too long 55 years of hurt

Remember lads you can do this you have three lions on your shirt

34.THE TREE

Oh, big oak tree Oh big oak tree

It could be him or it could be me

Feeling so low feeling like you are feeling

Wanting to go

So don't ignore someones cry for help

35 TEARS

When tears roll down your face

When you have lost someone

Just close your eyes

And imagine their face

Because nobody can erase the memories of those days

36 NEGATIVE FLOW

People in your life come and go

As I look back on this with a negative flow

Some of our loved ones

And friends in heaven

So sad to see them go

So, on New Year's Eve

Light those lanterns

And watch them go

Right up to the sky

To shine a light down you

Maybe they can see you you never know

37.A DREAM

I had a dream before I met you

A vision of a beautiful girl holding my hand

A slender frame

Who was walking in the sand

I drew a heart with your name on it

It was fate

Our lives are mapped out

You cannot plan

But iv got to rmber treat her right I am a lucky man

38.SILENCE

When she looks into my eyes

They speak to me

She doesn't have to open her mouth

She doesn't have to part her lips

The words I see in her eyes

They sparkle like diamonds

In her eyes I can't help but stare

They hypnotise

I forget my troubles my cares

I hope forever now she is mine shes going nowhere

39.A REAL MAN

A real man should have a girls back

No matter what she is going through

No matter how long it takes

He gives her time and space

He will sit back and wait

Because in his heart she always has a place

40 tears

Sat here laughing tears rolling down my face

These are not tears of joy they are tears of pain

Sometimes you hide it well

Something has to take the strain from a broken heart.

Part 2 .Poetry of The People

The hurt inside.

When you hurt deep inside.

The gap between love and hate.

Is not so wide.

I distance myself .

You took my pride

I will never get that back

The old me died!.

Ninety nine.

Even if I am 99.

I will wait till you say you love me .

And you are mine!.

Many scars.

She has many scars

She is my star

She lights up my dark

I want to heal her broken heart

Shes my jigsaw piece

The beat to my heart.

My princess.

She is my girl with the golden crown.

I never want to let her down.

She is a living angel.

She is one of a kind .

She is tattoed on my mind.

Our hearts entwined.

The love of my life.

Potential wife.

I want to be there through thick and thin.

I want all her troubles all her strife

To her I would truly dedicate my life

5.Princess.

Some princesses don't wear a crown.

Some angels are here on earth.

Some girls deserve the world.

6. Enchanted.

She smells sublime.

The scent of this woman.

Has penetrated my soul.

She has taken my heart.

Hope one day she is mine.

Well that is my goal.

7. Love and money.

If money could buy love .

I would buy yours!.

8 .Gods angel.

God sent me an angel to save my soul.

9. Scared

I was scared to live again.

Until I saw an angels face.

10. Scars

I can see her scars .

But they make her perfect .

It makes her who she is .

I want to fix her heart.

She is so perfect   .

She is my missing part.

11. One in a million.

She is one in a million.

A rare find.

The love of my life.

Maybe I can get her to love me one day

Make her my wife.

12.ode to the ex.

She don't like me fighting back.

Dragging myself up.

When you had me on my knees.

With nothing but my shoes.

No home nothing to lose.

Now she is bitter and twisted.

Because I am on the up.

I am on the mend.

I got myself a house my home.

Some friends .

Some nice clothes.

She has failed.

She sends messages .

her bitterness shows!.

13. Abuser.

On the inside I scream.

On the outside its silence.

Too scared to speak out.

Yours anonymously .

A victim of domestic violence.

14. What she means .

What she means to me words cannot say.

My heart belongs to her it is there to stay.

She was the only one there for me.

The only one that cares for me.

When I needed.

When my soul was dead.

When my heart bled.

Thanks to her I am again alive.

She doesn't know what she did.

She re energised my heart.

She put me back in a good place.

She is kind hearted.

Not just that perfect face.

A warm hearted soul.

She is a diamond cut to perfection.

In her mirror everyday a beautiful reflection.

She has it in her eyes .

The look nobody can describe.

She was my medicine

That nobody could prescribe.

I cure for my broken heart.

She has built me up bit by bit.

Piece by piece .

She has fixed my heart .

I am no longer lost I owe her .

15.Dark place

I am in a dark place.

Someone turn on the light.

I am walking down a never ending tunnel.

No end in sight.

Imagine a maze with no exit or end.

Trapped is how I feel.

Depressions not my friend.

16. old me

The old me was happy.

The old me was kind.

The old me had love in his heart.

Not empty and sad .

With a bitter mind.

17. crowded room

Feeling alone in a crowded room.

It consumes you.

Clouds your views.

I look at people .

Ignoring their voices.

Staring straight through.

I don't want to be there.

I panic.

I don't know what to do.

Shall I stay or leave .

I am too scared to talk to you.

One more hour I stay .

Because being this anxious is hard to do .

18 a smile

A smile can hide a heart that is broken.

A smile can hide hurtful words that are spoken.

The pain inside is what nobody can see.

One day I hope all the pain is gone.

And I am finally set free.

Allowed to live again .

Allowed to be the old me.

19. raging fire

A raging fire in my soul.

She made me feel whole.

She took my heart.

But she was so so cold.

Her frozen heart.

She knows how to play games.

She knows how to blame.

How to point the finger.

I will never be the same.

This is the end for me she has killed my soul.

20.Curtains

The curtains are drawn staring at the wall.

Along came my super hero.

She got me through it all.

The smile on her face was enough to get me by.

I here today she is the reason why.

Her words that she whispered .

They really meant the world.

She doesn't know what she means to me this girl.

I owe her my life.

Because of her I must confess.

Without her care.

I was truly a mess.

She is my rock.

21 A BROKEN GIRL.

Such a beautiful girl .

On her shoulders the weight of the world .

A fake smile her makeup done.

Her hair straight .

Her beauty glows deep

inside.

Lots of woes buy hey that her life.

That how her depression grows.

Maybe one day she will speak out.

When her confidence grows.

Do not judge her as she is like a delicate flower .

In time she will be ready to tell you .

From the heart how she is truly feeling.

She might let you in that a start.

As you don't know how she feels.

What caused the heartache?.

Who has abused her who caused the heartbreak?.

Who smashed her confidence?.

What took it away? .

This girl is a battler she fights everyday.

To keep alive.

To keep going for the sake of her sanity .

I guess the moral to this poem .

Is to not judging her purely on her vanity.

22 HER EYES.

Her eyes stand out like shining jewels.

Her silk like hair flowing in the wind.

A beautiful colour that compliments her skin.

Her eyes so deep you could fall into them.

22 Beauty

Red hair.

Like the flames of desire .

Longing for her touch.

Her eyes have so much natural beauty .

When she awakens in a morning.

It reminds me of a flower .

Opening its tiny petals .

For the first time in spring.

23. I LONG FOR HER.

The one I long for has depth in her soul.

Her beauty is much more than physical.

She has beauty within .

She has an amazing glow .

From her smile to her half cut top.

That shows her dainty navel .

To her sublime curves .

To the tiny spot near her toe .

Everything about this girl.

Her silken hair .

The way she walks with elegance and grace .

Perfection!.

24. THE ONE.

You know they are the one .

When you only have to see their face.

To make you smile.

When you go to bed at night.

You know its all worthwhile .

When you look in her eyes.

You know youre truly complete.

25. DATING GAME.

Love these days.

Is the way you look .

Its what car you drive.

It is all about how much you can give.

It is what you can offer.

26. SWIPE LEFT SWIPE RIGHT.

Swipe right swipe right.

All based on vanity.

The six packs the abs .

Have you lost your sanity.

27. LOVE.

Love should be about holding hands.

A walk in the park.

Giving her flowers.

A kiss on the cheek.

Treating her special making her knees go weak.

If you are treating her right her beauty will glow.

If you carry this through her smile will be wide.

The surest thing is she will be yours for keeps.

She will never leave your side.

28. DARK LOVE.

I was living in the dark.

I had broken my heart.

But out of the dark ..

It soon turns to light.

You have to live again.

A girl will soon come along .

To relight the fire.

To awaken your soul.

29. IM HURT.

You have been hurt .

You build walls.

You put of defences.

You will never let down your guard.

Nobody can tear down those fences.

You are staying single.

Just you and the kids .

You want no man.

That is your preferences

You will not take the risk

scared to get your hurt again

30. MENTALY SCARRED.

Woman- do not touch me!

Man-gave her a kick!

Woman-what gives you the right thats sick!

Man-punches her in the face!

Woman-on her knees covered in blood!

Man-ill change don't leave I said I would!

Woman-bags packed im leaving you for good!

She has gone mentally scarred!

31. LOVE A WOMAN.

If you really love a woman

Treat her with kindness

Not hurtful tears or neglect

Give her respect

Cherish her heart and soul.

32. DROWNING.

Feel like I am drowning again

You are pushing me under

The day will come

No more lightening no more thunder

Bring me sunshine

That will be cool

No more hurt no more men no more the fool!

No more treating me cruel!.

33. THE WEDDING POEM

Fate drew us together

Never to be apart

Since I first saw your face you really stole my heart

We will walk down the aisle aloving smile upon our face

Knowing deep inside our hearts have found their truly natural place

A tender touch

A glancing look

Our fast beating hearts

Once the rings are on our fingers thats when our wonderful new life together truly will start.

33.ABUSE

All these things cannot be confused

Hurt full words are abuse

Putting someone down is abuse

Lashing out at your partner is abuse

Speak up speak out get out don't tolerate abuse

34. longing.

I long for someone to say its ok

Too afraid to speak out

I want to get away

Frightened to tell because nobody believes you

Frightened they will deny it all all the things they did

Hoping one day somebody believes you

And that they will blow the lid

35.saying sorry

They say they are sorry

All is forgiven

Day after day your life isn't worth living

You stay for the kids

Your abuse is hidden

A smile on your face

When they come home from school

They come home from work you live by their rules

Thinking of that day you walk out

And suffer no more

The final time you walk through that door

36.love a woman

If you really love somebody

Treat them with kindness

Not hurt and tears

Cherish her heart and soul

37. She has gone!

Woman –do not touch me!

Man-gave her a kick

Woman-what gives you the right your sick!

Man –gave her a punch!

Woman-on her knees covered in blood!

Man-im sorry ill change

Woman-you said that before!

Man-ill change don't leave!

Man-I swore on my life ill change I told you I would!

Woman-bags packed left for good!

Man-serves him right!

37.Her eyes are a beautiful silence!.

She has a funny way of coming and taking my cares away.

One look in her eyes

They have so much to say.

She is silent.

A beautiful silence.

But her eyes speak loudly!.

38. Perfect to me.

Take one look at her hair.

Her eyes.

Her face.

A pefect example of the human race.

A girl with a heart.

She is so kind .

so bold.

The perfect body.

The perfect face.

I can get lost in her brown eyes.

Im trapped in the maze.

There so deep.

Like an ocean.

She walks so perfectly dainty

When she is in motion.

You get what you see.

No lies .

No dishonesty.

PERFECT to me!.

39.FRONTLINE WARRIORS SUPER HEROES

Lockdown.

Shutdown no beer

NO football no cheer

Shockdown!

No K.F.C. so what!

No SUBWAY!

No NANDOS !

No DOMINO!

Its for the best

No visiting family!

No visiting friends!

But not long now!

Hang fire!

Party time when this pandemic end!

But spare a thought for the N.H.S

Trying their hardest to stop those deaths!

Not all super heroes wear capes!

But super heroes none the less!

40. I miss you! .

I miss you ! .

I only wanted to kiss you .

I quit trying ! .

When you wasn't sure .

Your heart so pure.

My heart break needs a cure .

41. Losing you!

Loving you is easy.

Having to walk away

Is like someone

Putting their hand through

Your chest

And ripping your heart out.

42.My heart on fire.

She set my heart on fire

It burns with desire

Her beauty I have no choice

But to sit back and admire

She glows from deep inside

I wait with my arms open wide

I will wait for her

My love will not subside.

43. From the start

I loved you from the start

I did not mean to push you

I didn't want to lose your heart

I didn't want to rush you

Your my best friend

This really is so hard.

44.Pushing me away.

You can keep trying to push me away

But I am not going to go away

Because I am here unconditionally

In your heart everyday

I am here for you

Whenever you need me

Through the dark days.

45. Reborn.

My heart is torn.

My soul has died.

One day maybe.

Ill be reborn.

And live my life

Free of regrets.

46.My best friend.

I lost my best friend

I deeply regret

Every minute of the time we had

ill never forget

If I did her wrong

I am sincerely sorry

All I can do right now is sit and worry

But if she doesn't forgive me

There is nothing that can be done

I cannot wait forever

My heart will slowly heal

It will eventually move on

The laughs we had

The tears we cried

After one silly argument

Our friendship died

Maybe one day you will forgive and forget

But spending time with you

Ill never ever regret.

47.Losing someone.

Losing someone you love

Feels like a part of you died with them.

48.Heaven baby.

If it was not for you id be in heaven baby
There is something about you baby
That is just not going away
I can feel it in my heart
This is the way its going to play?
There is something about you girl
That makes me feel like this
My heart is aching baby
Its breaking baby Each and every day
Since i lost you
A part of me has gone away
There is a missing piece in my heart
That i can no longer find
You was my shining star
My only hope my sunshine ray

Now I am left all alone again

I am really hurting baby

We had something good goin on

But you Just threw my heart away

But i know it is all my fault

And what i did was wrong

But believe me now baby

That is why i wrote this

dont know if its wrong

I want to be with you once more

I really need you right now

But i got to be strong

Because losing you has ripped my heart out baby

Took me Right back to the start

When i was just an empty shell

You brought me back to life baby ,

Took me out of my personal hell .

Its really broke my heart

49.in her eyes .

When the sun begins to set and the moon begins to rise .i am thinking of the future and when i look at you i can see it in your eyes

50. Yesterday

Reaching back to yesterday

because your frightened of tomorrow

It cant sureley end this way

51.Lose to win.

some times you have to lose to win .I had to be a man take it on the chin . i didnt kniw what else to do . i would never have known real love if id missed out on you

52.a child's lock down

.When they said to me there would be no school me and my brother said great oh cool !. now six weeks have passed without an end .we really miss school and playing with our friends .we can't play out just stay inside or in the garden on our bikes we ride .so please mr Johnson i really wish you'd relax these lockdown rules. so i can back out and get back to school .i know its not safe just not quite yet but it really does make me anxious and fret that this is forever i know its not but im losing time playing out n I am driving my mum mad n she's losing the plot.

53. The girl I knew

The girl I once knew always made things right

The girl I once knew tonight is on her own

The girl I once knew I am waiting by my phone.

54.Hearts in bits

Heart in bits soul in pieces

Hearts in bits my soul in pieces .

She has moved on .

She's pulled the plug

She has her freedom .

And I am left grieiving .

She's Left me with nothing to Believe in .

I look ok but a broken heart can be hidden .

A smile can be deceiving.

55.Sat in the dark.

Sat in the dark drinking bourbon

Listeninng to my favourite band

A rejected heart thats lost its spark

Out of the shadows

Then she came to wake me soul

To fix my heart

Thought she was the one

I pushed it too far

she pulled the plug

Our friendship was done

You let me get close

That is what hurts the most

The hardest thing is to walk away

I never got to have a say

She is in control

Of my destiny

I built up trust

For the first time in years

If i hadn't said how i felt

My heart would have spontaneously combust

It was shit or bust

Now she knows how I am feeling

Her rejection had me reeling

Its down to her now

My hearts hit the floor

Its over now

our friendship is no more

the is no worse feeling..

56.I met you.

i met you !.

i met you

doubt ill ever forget you

youll forget me

i outed me feelengs

hope youll never regret me

i dont wanna play these games

i dont wanna burn in your flames

i crashed from the love i gave

my love you rejected

my life with you in it

was perfection

i saw my future with you

i opened upto you

there was no prevention

to the hurt i endured

for a heart that was broken

no magic potion

there is no cure

57. My heart.

my heart .

i would swim the deepest ocean

i would run the longest road

i would climb the highest mountain

just to be with you tonight

i would fly in stormy skies

i would run through the darkest jungles

i would get struck by lightening

i would meet the holy ghost

i would fight a thousand men

i would walk on broken glass

i would lie upon a bed of nails

find you the pot at the end of the rainbow

try to get you the holy grail

i would fly to the moon

just to see your face

i would die for you

if that is what it takes

just to see you again

for one more time

my heart does the talking

no need to explain.